A

National Constitution:

THE ONLY

ROAD TO NATIONAL PEACE.

A

National Constitution:

THE ONLY

ROAD TO NATIONAL PEACE.

A

NATIONAL CONSTITUTION:

THE ONLY

ROAD TO NATIONAL PEACE.

A LETTER

TO

THE PRESIDENT OF THE UNITED STATES.

By WILLIAM GILES DIX.

BOSTON:
ESTES AND LAURIAT,
143 Washington Street.
1875.

UNIVERSITY PRESS: WELCH, BIGELOW, & Co.,
CAMBRIDGE.

to national shoulders, it sought and yet seeks to extend and apply the cloth by a patchwork of amendments; but this patching, patching, everlasting patching, with amendments after amendments is not the work required. It is trifling with great needs, great opportunities, great responsibilities, and gives no sign or proof of those qualities which the world generally concedes to America, — energy and directness of thought and action.

The President's Message has some most commendable suggestions; but it is marked by the usual irresolution of his state papers. It lacks the tone of authority and decision which people expect and like to see in those whom they choose for their civil guides. Those rulers have ever been not only the most efficient, but the most honored, revered, and beloved, who have dared most plainly to say, and have most boldly dared to do, what was right, and what they knew to be right. Within the strict limit of his Constitutional duty, the President could have said more and done more to promote national unity as the only pledge of national safety and peace.

The President seems to regret the fading away of the lurid and distracting colors of Federalism, and to look with all the horror his nature permits upon the genial, growing light of nationality, which, notwithstanding his horror, will shine more and more, and brighter and brighter, unto the perfect day. It seems hopeless to expect him to begin, as he only can, by urging others to begin the great work of organic reform. In the faith and fear of God then I lift and unfurl the standard of a National Constitution, and implore my countrymen to rally around it, armed only with the wills and words of patriotic demand; for there will be and can be no safety for American unity, prosperity, power, and liberty, and there will be and can be no patriotic devotion, loyal and harmonious, from the Lakes to the Gulf, and from ocean to ocean, except under a National Government, ruling by the forms and sanctions of a National Constitution.

W. G. D.

PEABODY, MASS., *December* 29, 1874.

NATIONAL RECONSTRUCTION.

PEABODY, MASSACHUSETTS, October 1, 1874.

TO U. S. GRANT, *President of the United States.*

MR. PRESIDENT, — During the gloomy year of 1779, George Washington, in a letter to a friend, wrote these words of wisdom: —

"To me it appears no unjust simile, to compare the affairs of this great continent to the mechanism of a clock, each State representing some one or other of the smaller parts of it, which they are endeavoring to put in fine order, without considering how useless and unavailing their labor is, unless the great wheel or spring, which is to set the whole in motion, is also well attended to, and kept in good order."

In the same letter he had written as follows: —

"I have seen without despondency, even for a moment, the hours which America has styled her gloomy ones; but I have beheld no day since the commencement of hostilities, when I have thought her liberties in such imminent danger as at present. Friends and foes seem now to combine to pull down the goodly fabric we have hitherto been raising, at the expense of so much time, blood, and treasure; and unless the bodies politic will exert themselves to bring things back to first principles, correct abuses, and punish our internal foes, inevitable ruin must follow. Indeed, we seem to be verging so fast to destruction, that I am filled with sensations to which I have been a stranger until within these three months." *

The evil genius which nearly drove to despair the Father of his Country, and, more than anything else, hindered his heroic labors for the good of all, was State jealousy, the main cause of all the dangers and anxieties of the Revolution. The earnest appeals of

* Marshall's Life of Washington, Vol. IV. pp. 7-9.

George Washington could not wholly quell the spirit of State pride, which has been the curse of the country from the beginning. Even at that terrible period, when the union of wills, hearts, and hands was pre-eminently needed, the States, mutually jealous, were all jealous of the powers watched with suspicion and conferred with reluctance upon the General Congress. In that Congress itself some State often looked larger than all the rest of the struggling country, and no doubt often caused a narrow, unwise, and injudicious decision, or prevented one broad, wise, and beneficent. The bright prize of Independence at times grew pale before the blazing terrors of Continental unity.

Mr. President, I have quoted the words of George Washington, to point my rebuke of your failure to comprehend the real needs of the country over which you preside more like anything else than like an inspiring leader. You have especially failed to take a single step towards what the past, the present, and the future unite in demanding, — national consolidation. You were a directing general; you have been a drifting President. In your civil administration you have had the opportunities of a giant, and you have used them like a dwarf. At the head of our army, you often triumphantly flanked the enemy. At the head of our nation, your political foes and your political friends have taken turns in flanking you. As the commander in the field, you were determined to keep on the same line, if it should take all summer; you did so, and won for your country victory, and for yourself as a soldier imperishable fame. As our executive guide, so far from keeping on the same line, if it should take all summer, you have crooked and doubled like the Mississippi River, all the year round.

Mr. President, your countrymen have not known where to find you. You have had no fixed principles of civil rule. Your compass has been subjected to the influence of so many magnets, that the people could not tell your course, or whether you were true to it or not. They may well doubt whether you could tell yourself. You have, indeed, at times, maintained the national honor with something like the vigor of your military career; but there has been a preceding doubt, whether or not you would, so that your right action has been the source of grateful surprise. There should have been no occasion for the doubt, none for the surprise, however grateful.

Congress, at its last session, passed an act, which, dishonorable in its character, would have been disastrous in its effects. Before

deciding on your duty, you kept the country in an agony of suspense. At last you decided right, and your country thanked you for so doing; but there should have been no agony of suspense. Your countrymen should have had such thorough faith in your personal and official manhood, as to know as well what you would do, as, afterwards, what you had done. The ink was hardly dry on your Veto Message, when Congress passed another act, containing no recognition of the principle that nothing is money but money. You doubled on your own record, and approved the act; and nobody was surprised. You seem to prefer to make your course by tacking, even when the wind is fair. Nevertheless, your countrymen are apparently expected not only to show the utmost forbearance towards your shuffling, seesawing administration, during the rest of your term, but to take a third lease of your indifference to great and momentous questions, of your peculiar will, yielding and unyielding by fits and starts, and of your love of ease, which seems to be equal to your love of power,— power, I mean, for the name of it, not for the work of it. This is not the entertainment to which your countrymen were invited; certainly not the one which they accepted.

Mr. President, the indirections and vagaries of your administration have not proceeded wholly from your own will, but, to a great degree, from our theory and practice of government. The Republic of the United States of America tries to conduct a national business on a federal capital. The endeavor is a great trial in more than one way, and makes awkward work. Organized governments call our federation a nation by courtesy, and we are content with the courtesy, though we have not one national citizen within our borders, except as a citizen of one of the States may be adopted as a citizen of all the States. American citizenship goes by a roundabout road. No such being as an American citizen, meaning one of our own people, owing and paying single civil allegiance, lives in the wide world.

You came into the Presidential office at a time when a commanding statesman was wanted, one having the intuitive and instructed wisdom, and the invincible energy of thought and action, which make and mark the great statesman in all lands and in all ages. No such man was to be found. Your countrymen elected you, in the hope that you would be as straightforward as a political guide as you had proved as a military chief. Before the ceremonies of your inauguration were over, you disappointed

that reasonable hope. Five minutes after you took the oath of office, you were understood to renounce the character of a guide of the people, and to take that of their docile and obedient follower. Yet never was a guide more needed. You were chosen as a guide; and a guide it was alike your right and your duty to be. Washington was a guide, a faithful and fearless guide, blending, as President, the true, though stately courtesy of the Virginia gentleman with the unbending will, when he knew he was right, of the American ruler. Jackson was a guide, Lincoln was a guide. If you did not intend to be a guide, or knew not how to be a guide, why were you President?

You became President, in consequence of the national victory, in which you bore a share so honorable and eminent; but, Mr. President, let me entreat you to consider that it was a national, not a federal victory which you won; and that national victory signified the defeat of the Federal Constitution. This truth either you were not keen enough to see, or not bold enough to say. The surrender of General Lee was by the very act, and at the same instant, the capitulation of the Federal Constitution; yet, from that day to this, neither the ruling powers of the country, nor the people, have recognized the fact. While honoring you as heartily, as ardently, and as gratefully as you ought to be honored for your wise and noble work in bringing about that surrender, I wonder why, in your Inaugural Address, or, at least, in your first Message to Congress, you did not say that, while the Federal Constitution is binding upon all — not the rulers only, but the people also — while remaining the Constitution, nevertheless the evils and dangers of federalism had been demonstrated at a terrible sacrifice of heroic and loyal lives on one side, and by cruel displays of misguided bravery on the other; that the great results of the national victory could not be secured and made permanent except by eradicating federalism entirely and forever from all departments of the government, executive, legislative, and judicial; and that this should be legally done, according to justice and precedent, as soon as possible, by the consent of the people. In accepting the nomination for the Presidency, you said, no doubt, most sincerely and kindly, "Let us have peace"; but Slavery was not a greater foe to true national unity, than Federalism is to true national peace.

Mr. President, it was not wise to reconstruct the returning States on federal principles, though it was imperative to do so, if

the rest of the States were to remain federal. What was needed then was what is needed now, to reconstruct all the States on national principles. The State governments should be content with the patriotic duty of being the agents and representatives of the national government, instead of the general government being the agent of the States. The States, as federal actors, must soon make their final exit from the American stage. They have played in comedy and in tragedy. Their comedy attempting to combine the orderly and graceful movements of nationality with the ungainly gymnastics of federalism, has been the source of uncontrollable mirth. Their tragedy has been an astounding success. In its performance, shouts of exultation for the final triumph of the right were blended with agonies that could not be told; and tears, sighs, and sufferings continued long after the curtain fell. Let the States go, — let them go, with all their bloody robes around them, and, if they can, hide themselves forever from the sight of God and man; and, in their place, behold one powerful, pervading, Christian dominion, as broad as the continent, as bright as the sun, as enduring as time.

Mr. President, "the Rebellion" did not spring out of the theories, as theories, of John C. Calhoun. "The Rebellion" was a natural and logical growth from the Federal Constitution; and the same soil and the same tree may, in due season, bring forth the same fruit. Mr. Calhoun's theory, that the Constitution records and confirms the compact of a League of States, having a general agency for named duties, is more literally, logically, and historically correct, than Mr. Webster's theory, that it is the charter of a national government. The Articles of Confederation and the Federal Constitution differed in degree only, not in kind, both being federal, neither national. I know that Daniel Webster is said to have won, in the great Constitutional debate between federalism and nationality, a peaceful, complete, and enduring victory for nationality. I deny it. In the glare and roar of a hundred battles, where the same question was debated with flashing swords and thundering batteries, I fail to see the completeness, the endurance, or the victory. Daniel Webster's motive as "the Defender of the Constitution" was as noble, chivalric, and sublime as his genius, and his grand nationality of feeling, which beamed with unfading splendor to his dying hour, is worthy of unbounded and unending honor and praise, while he sleeps in a patriot's grave, blest by the brightness of a patriot's fame. But the gigantic power of the advocate, though flaming with the ardor of a great and glorious heart, made clearer the inherent weakness of the case.

A constitution cannot be called national, in any proper meaning of the word, when its nationality is the subject of inference and implication. True, avowed nationality is as plain and as bright as the sun, and needs neither the lamp of genius nor the microscope of logic to detect it. The nationality of a document which has been denied by some as persistently as it has been maintained by others for eighty years, with at least equal authority on the side of those who deny it, cannot be a very clear and direct nationality. It cannot be a very bright day, when one can take either side of the question, whether the sun is shining or not. The patriotism that has to be divided into nearly forty pieces lacks essential unity.

George Washington, Alexander Hamilton, George Read, James Wilson, Charles Pinckney, Rufus King, and other nationalists of the Constitutional Convention, who desired a national government more or less strong according to their individual views, but a national government as distinguished from a federal agency, were defeated in that Convention. Like good patriots they submitted; and, hiding as well as they could the Moses of Nationality in the bulrushes of Federalism, they accepted and even advocated a Federal Union, when they could not get national unity, and hoped for a brighter day. Time and a bitter war have triumphantly, though terribly, vindicated their patriotic wisdom and foresight. Let the American people also vindicate the patriotic wisdom and foresight of those noble but defeated men, in the enduring form of a National Constitution. This will not be to undo, but to fulfil, the work of our fathers.

Mr. President, as one of the people, I voted for you twice as a guide. You have refused to be one. But you said that you would have no policy to enforce against the will of the people. I hold you to your word. I believe that the American people, as soon as they shall see, and they cannot long help seeing, that the only bulwark in the power of man to build against another fierce and fearful war upon the national authority, in the North and in the South, is a National Constitution, rejecting federalism in all its disjointed joints and formless forms, and avowing nationality in all its harmony, beauty, and energy, will so plainly speak their minds, that you will be justified in urging upon Congress the right and the duty of appointing a time, as soon as may be deemed best, for delegates, chosen one for and by each Congressional district, but from any part of the country, to assemble in Philadelphia, — which the hopes of our fathers and the memories of their sons, meeting like the wings of the cherubim over the ancient altar of God, together consecrate as the Holy City of our history, whose inspirations light the loyal eye, cheer the loyal heart, and nerve the loyal arm, — there to consider and form a NATIONAL CONSTITUTION, not for a Federal Union of States, but for one great State, one only and one forever.

It must be understood that our National Constitution, when formed, is to be submitted for approval or rejection, not to the States, but to the people, as one people, and voting as one. From the beginning to the end of the work, the States, as States, must have nothing to do with forming or adopting a National Constitution. In this great work of a Constitution suited to the national unity, welfare, and glory, and intended to annihilate utterly and forever the shape and shadow of the gory demon of State-Sovereignty, I venture, in the name of my countrymen, to say to the States: *Hands off! you have done mischief enough.*

Mr. President, since you will not lead, I challenge you to follow. If you will not accept the challenge, then, if I shall live, I will do all that honorably and earnestly I can, to make *a National Government and a National Constitution* the watchwords of a triumphant National Party at the next Presidential election. But I hope that you are not willing to have your name handed down in American history, as that of a man who knew how to lead an army to victory, but knew not how, and had no desire, to complete and confirm that victory by leading the American people out of the Dismal Swamp of Federalism to the firm, wholesome, and beautiful domain of Nationality. I hope that you will so act that your Presidential career may honorably end, and that your successor's may happily begin, under the auspices of a National Constitution.

Mr. President, I have written with a determination, should this letter impress you or not, to do all that one man can, by earnest entreaty, to persuade my countrymen that a Federal Constitution, designed for and suited for a League of States, is not suited for a national domain, which may yet grow, until its boundaries and those of North America will be the same, but which cannot safely grow, or develop its organic life within its present limits, unless endowed with the central energy, expansive power, and glorious liberty of a National Constitution. Against whatever blame I may have to bear for expressing this opinion, I hold up as a shield the revered and precious name of George Washington, whose words quoted at the beginning of this letter were not more appropriate when written than now.

I quote these words from Washington's Farewell Address:* "The basis of our political systems is the right of the people to make and to alter their constitutions of government. But the constitution which at any time exists, until changed by an explicit and authentic act of the whole people, is sacredly obligatory upon all." Are the theory and practice of our government now harmonious? If they are, when, how, and where was the federal theory by due authority renounced; and when, how, and where did the nationality in practice by due authority begin? If the theory and practice are not harmonious, ought they not to be made so "by an explicit and authentic act of the whole people"?

It is neither wise nor patriotic to hide from ourselves the truth, and there is no truth plainer in American history than this, that the Federal Constitution has been "weighed in the balances" and "found wanting." The quoted words of Washington's letter were indeed written while the War of the Revolution was in progress; but the Articles of Confederation had been adopted by Congress, and, one must believe, had some combining influence before being in due form adopted by the States. After being so adopted, they more than kept the promise of their weakness, though being in advance of the powers first conferred upon the Continental Congress. History, if not exactly, is sometimes nearly repeated. Our country now stands in a somewhat similar position towards the Federal Constitution to that in which she stood, before its adoption, towards the Articles of Confederation. A step forward was needed then. A step forward is needed now.

Mr. President, you have recently shown a spirit worthy of your office, and of that persistent will which, in another sphere, worthily won the applause and the honors of your country. Thankfully and cordially good citizens have praised you; but the events in Louisiana illustrate the danger, on one side, of upholding national authority with nothing but a federal charter to sanction the proceeding, and the danger, on the other, of allowing the national authority to be defied and resisted because there is nothing but a

* Marshall's Life of Washington, Vol. V. p. 694.

federal charter to support it. As things now are, the federal authority cannot be used without a requisition from those who may be overpowered by the insurgents for the very purpose of preventing the constitutional requisition, or who may be as bad as the insurgents, or worse, and by their own disorder may have incited greater disorder. To state the fact is to state the danger.

For nine years these contradictions of reconstruction have continued. They will continue and increase, until the American people shall see, and shall act according to the sight, that a permanent pledge of peace and unity between the North and the South, the East and the West, can be found only, as far as depends upon the will of man, in a National Constitution. When the governors of the States, whether chosen by a popular vote or appointed, can, in either case, show as the sign of their authority, not the record of the State, but the broad seal of the national government, behind which is all the power of the nation, requiring no local demand for its use in danger, they will not be likely to be driven from their posts by local violence; and when elections in all the States shall be conducted by national rules of suffrage and registration uniform throughout the land and making bribery and the manipulation of votes national crimes punished by national laws, there will be less opportunity and less motive for electoral fraud.

The Nation cannot be sovereign, and the States also sovereign. One or the other must yield. The Nation cannot yield without giving up her inspiring past and her hopeful future. The States, by yielding their pretences of sovereignty, will win a grander and brighter prize than they surrender, in the common power, welfare, and glory of one great and noble nation. The needed reconstruction must be thorough in character and in extent. It will not promote peace or patriotism to make half the States national, and to keep half the States federal. Our country must be one, literally one.

Mr. President, with this public letter to you begins, but here, by the aid and blessing of God, will not and shall not end, my work in behalf of a National Constitution, the harbinger of a thousand years of benignant power and brightening glory for our country, through whose darkest days have glanced the smiles of Heaven, while the batteries of mortal might have attacked in vain her towers of Almighty defence.

I am a stranger to you personally, yet not a stranger to your well-won fame. I have felt just pride, as an American, in what you did to make our brave national soldiers victorious; but I have felt humiliation, as an American, that you have not comprehended, or seemed to care to comprehend, the historic meaning of the war in which you won so bright a name, — that you have not seen, or even seemed to care to see, the need, the duty, and the destiny of the country which, as a soldier, you served with such directness, persistency, and boldness of power, but which, as a statesman, you have too frequently served like a pendulum, swinging between indecision in great things and firmness of will in little things. The American people will take good care how they again make a soldier their President, unless he has been charged with civil duties, and has shown in them energy, decision, and unity of purpose. In demanding a National Constitution, I plead for the whole country, for the protection of the South against internal disorders, and the corruption and tyranny of men unfit to rule, to whatever party they may belong, as well as for the security of the North against another federal insurrection.

Mr. President, because I have rebuked you for your narrow views of public duty, for your want of inspiring energy in civil government, and for being content to be a federal follower, when the very qualities and services which made you President, and the needed inauguration of a new era of power and glory for America, required you to be a national guide, I am none the less, but the more, and for this very reason,

Faithfully yours,

WILLIAM GILES DIX.

A PETITION FOR A NATIONAL CONSTITUTION.

THE undersigned, a citizen of Massachusetts, believing that the time has come, in the providence of God, when the people of the United States ought, once for all, to decide whether or not they desire and mean to be one sovereign nation, claiming the direct allegiance of all, and directly guarding the rights of all, makes his respectful petition, that the Senate of the United States, in concurrence with the House of Representatives, will appoint a time, as early in the coming year as may be deemed best, for delegates chosen one for and by each Congressional district, but from any part of the country, to meet in the city of Philadelphia, to consider and form a National Constitution, which, if approved by the people, voting as one people, without the intervention of the States, shall be declared by the executive authority to be, from a time named, the organic national law, superseding the Federal Constitution of the United States, as that Constitution superseded the Articles of Confederation.

WILLIAM GILES DIX.

PEABODY, MASS., December 1, 1874.

PEABODY, MASSACHUSETTS, December 25, 1874.

TO THE CONGRESSIONAL COMMITTEE ON THE REVISION OF THE LAWS.

GENTLEMEN, — The motive for my petition for a National Constitution, recently referred to you by the Senate, is, first of all, through all, and last of all, the desire of peace, enduring peace, of that peace which comes from unity of government, accepted by a loyal and united people. I mean no vindictive threat, no wayward display of national power.

The double civil allegiance, not only permitted, but required by the Constitution, has been the unfailing spring of political irritation and conflict to this hour. The makers of the Constitution, in trying to avoid the danger of unity, incurred the greater danger of the ruin of all their hopes and labors for union. They are not to be blamed for doing as they did. But few members of that Convention desired a thorough national government, and, though in the history of recent years the patriotic wisdom of those few shines brightly through their defeat, yet, had they prevailed in the Convention, their work, however inspired by genius and foresight, would have been rejected by all the States. Nationality was then an object of almost universal terror. The members of the Convention, representing independent States, were obliged to follow Solon's rule, and make such an organic law as the people could bear. In judging how far to go, and where to stop, they showed consummate and patriotic skill.

I cannot agree with those who regard the Constitution as a Charter of Nationality. In my belief it is a Federal Charter. It is an advance beyond the Articles of Confederation, but an advance on the same federal line. A national feature here and there may modify, but cannot entirely change, the general character of the Constitution, as the Charter of a Federal Union, not of National unity.

We cannot at all times, if we would, avoid acting as a nation; for behind all possible organizations stand the principles intended to be organized, and behind these are primal principles, which cannot be organized by the power of man; and all the objects to which those principles may be applied cannot be defined beforehand. No mortal form can be a perfectly faithful mirror of an immortal idea; and such is government; and even a federal agency is government, and, being government, as well as a government, must have some rights derived from a source above and before itself, independent of itself, and unchanging in its essential nature through all the changes of time.

I greatly doubt whether it is within the province of a Constitution to define in detail the special objects of a government, excluding all others. At any rate, I deny that a government the objects of which are so defined and restricted is a national government. The objects of a government seem to be entirely within the province of laws. A constitution of government may properly declare principles, prerogatives, immunities, and rights, and how they are to be applied and maintained, without making an exact inventory of the objects which, and which alone, they concern.

But, since the Federal Constitution attempts, and by so attempting is deprived of the claim to found a national government, to define and enumerate the special objects, and those only, which the government it forms can touch, it would be impossible in theory, and it has proved impossible in practice, always so clearly to draw and interpret the line of authority as to avoid censure and hostility for objects right in themselves, and admitted by their adversaries to be right, but which may not clearly lie within the limits of the granted powers. Sometimes strict construction, sometimes liberal construction, prevails. Many a wise law has been wrecked on a rocky comma in the Constitution, while many a foolish one has safely run the gantlet of all its pelting periods.

The greater the need of action, the more urgent the occasion, the greater the danger of overstepping the Federal boundary, the greater the danger that the discordant claims will culminate in unconstitutional resistance on one side, or in unconstitutional power on the other, or in both. I propose, then, a National Constitution, that this cause of never-ending irritation may be removed; that the theory and practice of our government may correspond, and that both may be national. I believe that many acts of the government, wise and just, are resisted upon the point of honor, because they are deemed, in the spirit if not in the letter, usurpations in a federal government, which would receive hearty and ready acquiescence, were the government avowedly, and by the consent of the people, national.

The same irritating conflicts — none the less irritating, and none the less conflicts, whether their causes were just or unjust, arising from real or presumed needs of national action — which brought on the civil war are now at work. The wisest statesmanship, the purest patriotism, cannot prevent the conflicts of divided authority — authority divided not by caprice or custom, but by organic law — which must inevitably come, not only from the endeavor to administer a federal government on national principles, but even from the most sincere endeavor to administer it on federal principles. Some "strict constructionists" have been Presidents, and have seen and owned the intense embarrassment of their position. Is it wise, is it straightforward, is it American, to go on, for all time, trying to give a National meaning to a Federal Constitution? I cannot think it to be so; and that is why I propose a National Constitution.

I do not believe that nullification and secession are justified by

the Constitution; but I plainly believe and plainly say, that so far as the Constitution alone is the basis of our political power, the theories of nullification and secession are not a greater strain, on one side of the Constitution, beyond the limit of allowed resistance, than the theory of a single, thorough, organic nationality is, on the other side, beyond the limit of allowed authority.

I know that many pure patriots have affirmed, and now affirm, the nationality of the Constitution; but many pure patriots have also denied it, and now deny it. Our nationality, so far as it depends upon the Constitution, is at least doubtful; and no vehemence of affirmation can make it logically or historically otherwise. Can a great nation, destined to be, if true to herself, to her trials, her opportunities, and her gifts of God, a controlling power in the world, be founded on a doubt as a corner-stone? Can we be truly a nation, in our own view or in that of others, when our nationality is not universally admitted by ourselves, but is by some doubted, by others denied, and by others denied and defied?

Gentlemen, behold for yourselves the dangers which will endure, and cannot help enduring, as long as the Federal Constitution shall be our organic law. We are bound by it while it shall remain; but does not every day bring warning that we must go forward and occupy national ground, if we would fulfil the work of our fathers, if we would vindicate the past, improve the present, and be just to the future? Can we be a harmonious people, when out of the very Constitution under which we live spring discords fierce and frequent?

I see the black cloud arising in the sky, like that which before burst upon the land; and, as it grows larger and blacker, and its shadow deeper and wider, I would connect the key of safety which shall draw powerless to the earth the fiery bolt, turn aside the lurid flame, so that its bright arrows of wrath may not again kindle civil strife on ripening harvest-fields, and so that the loud thunder, not again sounding the knell of death to many a manly heart and the knell of desolation to many a loving home, may bellow harmless to the vacant air. That key of safety is a National Constitution.

I see my country going on the same road which led to the terrible war. One after another appears each familiar milestone of danger. I venture, impelled by the sorrows of the past, and beckoned by the glories of the future, to stand in the way, and, in the name of God, of justice, and of right, to point out the sure high-road of a National Constitution, and to urge my country, letting go her heavy weight of conflicting authorities and discordant prerogatives, to advance on that firm, straight, and sunny road, like Pilgrim when he had lost his load of sin, in joy and liberty and peace.

Gentlemen of the Committee, I assure you, and reassure you, on this day, hallowed by the coming of the Prince of Peace, that my plea for a National Constitution springs from my ardent desire for peace, for national peace, for Christian peace, for peace as broad as our land and as bright as its hopes, for peace that shall cheer every American heart, bless every American home, defend every American's liberty and life, deck with unfading flowers every American patriot's grave, and make our American government, in all that concerns political right and loyal duty, the light of the world.

Can we doubt that our fathers, with our trials of Federal dangers added to theirs, would have made, with eager alacrity, a National Constitution? Can we doubt that it would have been adopted with eager acclamation by a united people? The way to follow our fathers and to honor their memory is to be as true to our day and our duty, with the light we have, as they were true to their day and their duty, with the light they had.

Gentlemen, however widely you may differ one from another, or from me, I believe that we shall all agree in hoping that our country may be, for benignant ages, one happy, free, and powerful dominion, the home of the brightest hopes and of the best endeavors, and a sanctuary alike of the unalienable rights of man and of the unalienable rights of God.

In this hope and belief, I am, Gentlemen, with great respect,

Very truly yours,

WILLIAM GILES DIX.

www.ingramcontent.com/pod-product-compliance
Lightning Source LLC
LaVergne TN
LVHW011142110826
845150LV00008B/2473

* 9 7 8 1 4 1 8 1 9 2 0 1 3 *